THE 7 HABITS OF Highly Effective Teens

Mini-Workbook

SEAN COVEY

CONTENTS

PART 1
The Set Up

Throughout this workbook there are questions to answer, small writing assignments (don't stop now – these are NOT like homework), ideas to expand upon. In the print version of the workbook we encourage you to write right in the book. We've provided space for answers and blank pages for additional thoughts and ideas.

LEARN   the 7 Habits

⊙ Use the highlight function or a highlighter to mark parts you want to remember.

⊙ Memorize quotes.

⊙ Study the workbook and think through the questions and concepts.

⊙ Make the learning fun.

LIVE the 7 Habits

⊙ Personalize and apply each habit to your life.

⊙ Challenge yourself to move out of your comfort zone.

⊙ Commit to do the Baby Steps at the end of each chapter in the book.

SHARE the 7 Habits

⊙ Discuss with a friend, parent, guardian, or teacher the ideas that are important to you.

⊙ Share with someone you trust the commitments or ways you want to change.

To get the most from **The 7 Habits Of Highly Effective Teens**, you have to make an investment. It will require time and commitment. Take a few minutes and glance through both the book and this workbook. Look at the pictures and read the headlines and quotes that interest you. Begin to get an idea of what this book is all about and what you might "get" from reading it.

After browsing the pages of the book and workbook, use the Notes feature to jot down your personal expectations and what you hope to learn.

Personal Expectations:

From reading **The 7 Habits of Highly Effective Teens,** I hope to be able to:

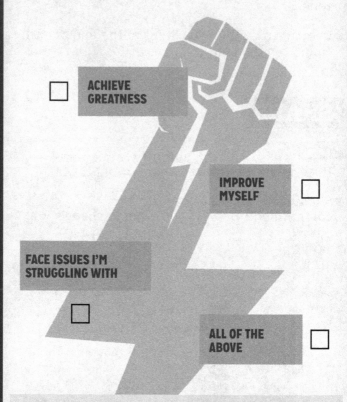

☐ **ACHIEVE GREATNESS**

IMPROVE MYSELF ☐

FACE ISSUES I'M STRUGGLING WITH

☐

ALL OF THE ABOVE ☐

Something to think about:

Did you check All of the Above? If you did, great job! That is the sort of positive thinking that leads to success. However, if you were hesitant, it's okay. What caused your hesitation? What do you hope to be able to do?

Get in the Habit

Habit 1: Be Proactive®
Take responsibility for your life.

Habit 2: Begin with the End in Mind®
Define your mission and goals in life.

Habit 3: Put First Things First®
Prioritize, and do the most important things first.

Habit 4: Think Win-Win®
Have an everyone-can-win attitude.

Habit 5: Seek First to Understand, Then to Be Understood®
Listen to people sincerely.

Habit 6: Synergize®
Work together to achieve more.

Habit 7: Sharpen the Saw®
Renew yourself regularly.

NOW THINK THE OPPOSITE WAY:

Take a look at each of the habits separately. If you need to flip back, go ahead. I'll wait. Now think about the opposite of each statement. What would it be? More importantly, what type of results would the opposite produce in your life?

Need a little help? Take a look at Habit 1: Be Proactive. The opposite of proactive is reactive. What type of results would you achieve in your life if you were always reacting? Do you see the power in the difference? Now come up with your own defective definitions for the other six habits.

(If you need more help, refer to p. 7 of The 7 Habits of Highly Effective Teens book).

Write Your Response Here.

Paradigms & Principles

What You See is What You Get

PARADIGM:
The way you think about and see things.

With this definition in mind, let's play a game.

Close your eyes and think of your favorite genre of music. Try to listen to it in your head.

Using the Notes feature or this workbook, write down what it is about this type of music that speaks to you.

Once you've determined why you are drawn to this sound, put this book down and go speak with your parents, siblings, and friends. Find out their opinions on music.

Did your paradigm change after listening to the paradigms of others? Why or why not?

Write Your Response Here.

"PARADIGMS ARE LIKE GLASSES.

WHEN YOU HAVE INCOMPLETE PARADIGMS ABOUT YOURSELF OR LIFE IN GENERAL, IT'S LIKE WEARING GLASSES WITH THE WRONG PRESCRIPTION."

— SEAN COVEY

TAKE A GOOD LOOK AT THIS PICTURE. WHAT DOES IT LOOK LIKE TO YOU?

WHAT DO YOU SEE? WHAT HELPED YOU COME TO THIS CONCLUSION?

Now look at this more complete version of the image from the previous page:

Is the picture what you thought it was? If not, you just experienced a paradigm shift – the way you saw something, your point of view, changed.

Some of our paradigms are about life in general. You can usually tell what your paradigms are by asking yourself "What is my life centered on?"

Write Your Response Here.

Before we move on, use this circle:

Look at the border. This border will serve as a divider.

Outside of the circle place all the things you spend your time on: friends, school, music, movies, sports...

Use the Notes feature or this workbook to write these things down. We'll come back to them shortly.

Refer to p. 25.

PRINCIPLE:
A natural law or basic truth
(i.e., honesty, service, love).

MENTAL QUIZ

Principles Never Fail.

They apply equally to everyone. They aren't up for debate. They can't be bought or sold. If you live by them, you will excel. If you break them, you will fail (hey, that sorta rhymes). It's that simple.

Think of a few examples of important principles. I'll help you get started:

- ⊙ Integrity
- ⊙ Hard Work
- ⊙ Loyalty
- ⊙ Responsibility

Can you think of some more? There are dozens. Don't worry! You don't have to list dozens. Just trust me on that.

Remember the circle from earlier? The one with the divider? Inside of the circle, insert the word "principle." Using the Notes feature or this workbook, write a few principles you admire.

Write Your Response Here.

What principles do you want to center your life around? It takes commitment to live by principles. But it's worth it! A principle-centered life is simply the most stable, immovable, unshakable foundation you can build on, and we all need that.

PART 2
The Private Victory

THE PERSONAL BANK ACCOUNT

"IF YOU HAVEN'T FORGIVEN YOURSELF SOMETHING, HOW CAN YOU FORGIVE OTHERS?"

— DOLORES HUERTA

A Private Victory is self-mastery; It's winning the battles within yourself.

The first three habits deal with the Private Victory. Can you name them? It's okay if you need to flip back. No one's grading your recall. Okay, did you find them? Did you review them? What do you think? How do the first three habits help you win battles within yourself?

It's about self-discipline, right?

LET'S PLAY A GAME

What have you done lately to exercise self-discipline? Maybe you decided to exercise more? Eat better? Wake up the first time your alarm clock goes off? Complete homework on time? Or maybe you've decided to control your temper?

Whatever you've done lately to exercise self-discipline, keep doing it. Repetition is a great friend as you develop better habits. So, here's the game: for the next three weeks (21 days), pick something you've already started or want to start and keep doing it.

If you miss a day, don't worry! Don't give up! Restart the 21 day clock and keep going. You're going to accomplish something amazing within yourself.

Habit: ....

Start date: ....

The personal bank account

Do you have a personal bank account? Or even a favorite spot under your mattress? Somewhere you put money, let it accumulate, and only withdraw when you need something?

How you feel about yourself is like a bank account. Just like a checking or savings account, you can make deposits or even withdrawals by the things you think, say, and do. When I stick to a commitment I've made to myself, it's a deposit. If I break a promise to myself, I feel disappointed and it's a withdrawal.

Consider the model below. What does your personal bank account look like? How can you make even more deposits? Can you use this form to track your personal bank account for a week?

Can I suggest some personal bank deposits? Do a small act of kindness. Be gentle with yourself. Be honest. Renew yourself. Tap into your talents. Refer to p. 35.

DESCRIPTION OF DEPOSIT /WITHDRAWAL	–	+	BALANCE
Stood up for something I believe		$75	$75
Read a book just for fun		$25	$100
Accepted myself as I am		$100	$200
Gossiped about a friend	$75		
Week total:	$75	$200	$125

WEEK: ....

DESCRIPTION OF DEPOSIT /WITHDRAWAL	—	+	BALANCE

What will your total be?

Refer to pp. 34-35.

Habit 1:
Be Proactive

I AM THE FORCE

"I AM THE CAPTAIN OF MY LIFE. I CAN CHOOSE MY ATTITUDE. I'M RESPONSIBLE FOR MY OWN HAPPINESS OR UNHAPPINESS. I AM IN THE DRIVER'S SEAT OF MY DESTINY, NOT JUST A PASSENGER."

— Sean Covey

Being proactive is the opposite of being reactive. It means to take responsibility for your actions. It means you refuse to be acted upon and controlled by events, your emotions, and the emotions and behavior of other people.

THINGS TO THINK ABOUT:

What is an example of a proactive choice you have made?

Write Your Response Here.

Refer to p. 51.

The language game

Below are various examples of reactive and proactive terms. Use the highlight function or a highlighter to mark the proactive phrases.

Refer to p. 51.

Think about your own language. Is it proactive or reactive? Each day, you and I have about 100 chances to choose whether to be proactive or reactive. What will you choose today?

LET'S TAKE THE PLUNGE!

You can Be Proactive! Here are a few ways to start Habit 1 today!

- Over the next week, keep track of your language, actions, and choices. Write down both the good and poor choices and actions you make on a day-to-day basis.

- Update this workbook and capture your feelings, thoughts, and ideas as you read through **The 7 Habits of Highly Effective Teens**.

- Baby Steps: Follow the Baby Steps at the end of each chapter of the book, starting with p. 28.

The
DO YOU
quiz

1

Do you believe you can make great things happen?

YES   NO

2

Do you think about positive solutions and options when faced with a choice?

YES   NO

3

Do you typically act instead of waiting to be acted upon?

YES   NO

Evaluate yourself!

Take time each day to ask:

⊙ Am I being proactive or reactive?

⊙ Did I make good choices today?

⊙ Did I blame someone else?

⊙ What language did I use?

Give an example of a great choice you made this week. What did you learn from it?

Write Response Here.

Habit 2:
Begin with the End in Mind

Begin with the End in Mind allows you to live your life with hope and purpose.

"THINK ABOUT YOUR OWN LIFE. DO YOU HAVE AN END IN MIND? DO YOU HAVE A CLEAR PICTURE OF WHAT YOU WANT TO BE ONE YEAR FROM NOW? FIVE YEARS FROM NOW? OR ARE YOU CLUELESS?"

– SEAN COVEY

Choices are awesome! Are you trying to make choices in your own life? What crossroads are you at in your life?

Following are some common questions teens ask themselves:

- ◉ Will I continue seeing only one person or do I want to start dating others?

- ◉ Should I get a job, get a new job, or stay where I am currently employed?

- ◉ Do I want to go to college or get into a vocational training program?

Think of some crossroads you expect to encounter in the next few months.

List the crossroads you think you'll encounter in the next few months.

MIRROR BREAK

Let's reach that future! To determine where you're headed, ask yourself the following questions:

What qualities do I want to develop in my life? Give an example.

What contributions do I want to make to others and my community? Give an example.

What things will I need to have for the kind of future I want? Give an example.

To begin with the end in mind, you must know where you want to go, who you want to be, and what you want to achieve in life. So why not put it in writing?

PERSONAL MISSION STATEMENT

A personal credo or motto that states what your life is about.

The Great Discovery™ is a fun activity designed to help you get in touch with your deeper self as you prepare to write a mission statement. Walk through it and answer the questions honestly in the space provided.

Step 1 – THINK

Think of a person who made a positive difference in your life. What qualities does that person have that you would like to develop?

Step 2 – IMAGINE

Imagine yourself in 20 years. You are surrounded by the most important people in your life. Who are they and what are you doing?

Step 3 – RISK

If a steel beam (six inches wide) were placed across two skyscrapers, for what would you be willing to cross? A thousand dollars? A million? Your pet? Your brother? Fame? Think carefully.

Step 4 – TIME

If you could spend one day in a great library studying anything you wanted, what would you study?

List ten things you love to do. It could be singing, dancing, listening to a podcast, drawing, reading, daydreaming – anything you absolutely love to do.

1

2

3

4

5

6

7

8

9

10

Step 6 – INSPIRATION
Describe a time when you were deeply inspired.

Step 7 – 1 PERSON
If you could spend an hour with any person who ever lived, who would it be? Why that person? What would you ask?

Step 8 – THE FUTURE
Five years from now, your local paper does a story about you and they want to interview three people – a parent, a brother or sister, and a friend. What would you want them to say about you?

Step 9 – SYMBOLISM
Think of something that represents you – a rose, a song, an animal. Why does it represent you?

Step 10 – TALENTS
Everyone has one or more talents. What are your talents? Highlight your list of talents. Choose from our list or add your own using the Notes feature or this workbook.

Numbers	Speaking
Words	Writing
Creative Thinking	Dancing
Athletics	Listening
Making Things Happen	Singing
Sensing Needs	Music
Mechanical	Trivia
Artistic	

Write Your Talents Here.

You've just taken steps on The Great Discovery! You've thought about who you are. You've listed what you value most. The steps on this path have helped spark ideas about your personal mission statement.

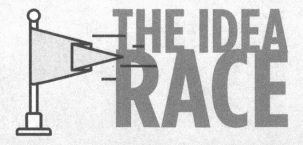

Now let's start to write one. What do you want your personal mission statement to include? Review your answers on The Great Discovery. Set five minutes on the clock and write all of the ideas that come to your mind during this time.

ON YOUR MARK. GET SET. GO!

> **Write Your Response Here.**

Don't worry if your mission statement is not perfect at first. Work on it over the next few weeks – add more ideas if you want. Once you've got it where it truly inspires you, put it where you can read it often. Need help?
Refer to pp. 81-82 and 91.

Habit 3:
Put First Things First

THE POWER OF WILL and WON'T

"THINGS WHICH MATTER MOST MUST NEVER BE AT THE MERCY OF THINGS WHICH MATTER LEAST."

— JOHANN WOLFGANG VON GOETHE

Give examples of the activities of each type of time manager.

THE EXAMPLE
GAME

What are traits of a:

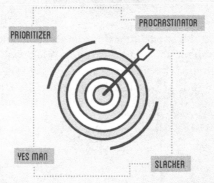

PRIORITIZER

PROCRASTINATOR

YES MAN

SLACKER

PROCRASTINATOR	PRIORITIZER
YES MAN	SLACKER

Refer to p. 107.

TIME GAME

Where do you spend your time? In the box below, detail how you spent your time yesterday. What took up most of your time? School? Work? Homework? Texting? Reading? Sports? Gaming? Hanging out? How much time did you spend on these activities?

Yesterday:

Write Your Response Here.

Let's examine the notes on the previous page

⊙ Did the things that filled up your day matter most to you?

⊙ Where did you waste time?

⊙ Where were you the most productive?

THE TIME QUADRANTS

Label each square of the time quadrants with the name of the time manager (Procrastinator, Prioritizer, Yes Man, Slacker).

	URGENT	**NOT URGENT**
IMPORTANT		
NOT IMPORTANT		

Review the previous page to see how you spent your time yesterday. Transfer over the tasks into the quadrant above.

How many activities were focused on Quadrant 2? Write down other Quadrant 2 activities that would have helped you put first things first.

Refer to p. 112.

Courage Zone
Discussion

Think of a time when you acted in the face of fear and took a risk to move outside of your comfort zone. What did you learn?

Under what circumstances do you need to step outside of your comfort zone and exercise more courage?

What holds you back from moving into your courage zone?

How can you act more courageously?

Dive Into Habit 3!

Using the Notes feature or this workbook...

Review your mission statement. Think about what it means to you today. If you are not done with it, write the next draft.

Make a weekly plan. Remember to look at the big picture. Ask yourself if all of your big rocks are in place.

Plan daily. With a weekly plan in place, you can focus on your daily priorities, tasks, and appointments.

Make a list. Examine your biggest time wasters and commit to focusing your time on more important things.

Practice. Take time to work on a skill, talent or habit you want to improve. Perhaps today it will be to practice being a better listener or to improve an athletic skill.

This week, use the Notes feature or this workbook to keep track of all the times you have done something that was important to you, although you didn't really want to do it at that particular moment.

Review the Baby Steps on p. 128.

Here, Write The Important Things You Did.

PART 3
The Public Victory

THE RELATIONSHIP BANK ACCOUNT

"KEEP IN MIND
THAT THE TRUE MEASURE OF AN INDIVIDUAL
IS HOW HE TREATS
A PERSON WHO CAN DO HIM
ABSOLUTELY NO GOOD."

— ANN LANDERS

How would you define a
Public Victory?

PUBLIC
VICTORY:
**Success with other people; your ability
to get along with others.**

Find a Friend – for this activity, you'll need to involve a friend, parent, or guardian. Start the conversation by asking them what they think a Public Victory is. Once you have a better understanding of their views, speak to them about the Relationship Bank Account.

> Describe to them how the Relationship Bank Account works and why it is important.

Proof of Purchase Game

Craft your own Relationship Bank Account Deposit Slip. Get as creative as you like. However, make sure that your Deposit Slip includes the following:

- Date
- Deposit / Action
- Dollar Amount ($)
- Signature

Date

Deposit

$

Signature

Refer to pp. 132-133.

Make several copies of your Relationship Bank Account slip. Give one to anyone who makes a deposit with you. This is like a thank-you note and will let the person know the value of the deposit he or she made with you.

Habit 4:
Think Win-Win

The All You Can Eat Buffet

"ME LIFT THEE, AND THEE LIFT ME, AND WE'LL ASCEND TOGETHER."

— JOHN GREENLEAF WHITTIER

What is win-win?

WIN  WIN

> **THINKING WIN–WIN IS THE FOUNDATION FOR GETTING ALONG WITH OTHER PEOPLE.**

Write your definition of win-win thinking. Once you have your description, share it with a friend. Use examples from your own life.

Complete the following sentences using the Notes feature or this workbook.

Refer to pp. 147-154.

◉ It is hardest for me to think win–win when:

◉ It is easiest for me to think win–win when:

◉ When I practice win–win thinking, I enjoy the following benefits:

Now that you have a better understanding of win–win, let's look at the other side.

What is win-lose?

WIN **LOSE**

When people only want to win and don't care if others lose.

Using the Notes feature or this workbook, write about an experience where you had a win-lose mentality.

How did you feel? Would you do things differently now?

Write Your Response Here.

What is lose-win?

LOSE   WIN

When people allow others to win even when it means they lose.

Using the Notes feature or this workbook, write about an experience where you practiced lose–win or someone acted in a lose–win way toward you. How did you feel?

Write Your Response Here.

What is lose–lose?

LOSE   LOSE

When people believe that if they go down, then others must go down with them.

Using the Notes feature or this workbook, list some lose–lose examples from history or current news events.

> **Write Your Response Here.**

The following exercise will help you start living Habit 4.

List a specific situation that you may face in the next seven days that will require win–win thinking. It might be during a music lesson, at work, in a challenging class, or at home with your family. How will you prepare yourself to think win–win?

Write Your Response Here.

Later, record the experience as it actually happened. Write what the experience taught you about thinking win-win.

Habit 5:
Seek First to Understand, Then to Be Understood

....

"BEFORE I CAN WALK IN ANOTHER'S SHOES, I MUST FIRST REMOVE MY OWN."

....

— UNKNOWN

Habit 5: Seek First to Understand, Then to Be Understood means listen first, talk second; see things from another person's point of view before sharing your own.

When was the last time you tried walking in someone else's shoes? What was the experience like – actually trying to consider another person's point of view or idea before sharing yours?

Using the Notes feature or this workbook, describe what happened and what you learned.

Write Your Response Here.

DICTIONARY
GAME!

Write your own definition of the following listening styles:

◉ Spacing Out:

◉ Pretend Listening:

◉ Selective Listening:

◉ Word Listening:

◉ Self-Centered Listening:

◉ Genuine Listening:

Refer to pp. 168-171.

What is mirroring? It is repeating back in your own words what another person is saying and feeling. You don't judge or give advice.

Read the following statement:

"I feel so ugly. Nobody will ever ask me to prom!"

A mirroring response could be:

"It sounds like you are discouraged about not being asked to the prom."

Now try some of your own. Think of mirroring responses for each of the following situations.

1

"No, you are not going out tonight!"

How would you respond using the mirroring technique? Feel free to say it out loud, write it down using the Notes feature or inside this workbook.

2

"You said I was the only one you wanted to be with, but that's not what I heard!"

Now that you understand, you need to be understood. To be understood requires courage.

"Then to Be Understood": This half of Habit 5 requires the courage to speak up.

When do you have the most difficult time giving feedback to others? Why?

If you genuinely listen to another person, what happens when you then express your feelings, ideas, suggestions, or opinions?

When was the last time you kept your thoughts and feelings to yourself even though you really wanted to share them? Why didn't you share them? How did you feel about it?

Now that you have analyzed your actions, what can you do to improve your practice of the second half of Habit 5, "Then to Be Understood"?

Habit 6:
SYNERGIZE

"DIFFERENCES CHALLENGE ASSUMPTIONS."

– ANNE WILSON SCHAEF

Synergy is when two or more people work together to create a better solution than either could alone.

To build and create synergy, you have to look for it. You have to see that each individual is unique and value that uniqueness. Name some synergistic relationships in nature, in your school and in your home. For example, sequoia trees and the flight formation of geese both demonstrate synergistic relationships in nature.

See how many different people you can learn about by completing the Synergy Boxes exercise. Write six more descriptions on the next screen. Now, go and find people who match the descriptions and write their names in the appropriate box. See how many names you can write in each box during the next two days.

THE SYNERGY BOXES

Add the name of the person you met who fits this description

Writes Stories, Plays or Poetry

Speaks More Than One Language

An Excellent Athlete

Cooks Extremely Well

Plays a Musical Instrument

Enjoys Studying Plants and Animals

Completing the Synergy Boxes exercise shows the importance of diversity and how each person is unique. But what about you? How are you different from others?

Refer to pp. 183-184.

THINK. DISCUSS. ANSWER.

1

Some people love to be with groups of people. Some people like to spend much of their time alone. How do you prefer to spend your time? Why?

2

Some people are dreamers; they're always thinking of new possibilities, new ways of doing things. Some people are very practical; they like to study the world and know how to do things. Which type of person are you? Why?

3

Some people make decisions based on their feelings and how they think others might feel. Other people make decisions based on facts. How do you prefer to make decisions? Why?

4

Some people like their lives planned out and scheduled. Other people like to be surprised or just see what happens. Which way do you prefer? Why?

The High Way

The "high" way is finding a better solution than win-lose, lose-win, or lose-lose, and it always produces more.

For this game you'll need to use the Notes feature or write in this workbook.

⊙ Keep track of an important issue that you, your community, your school, or your family is facing right now. Maybe it's violence at school, a dress code, or a community issue, such as changing the curfew for teenagers.

⊙ Organize a group of four or more people to discuss the issue you chose. Individually, think of ways to improve or change the problem.

⊙ Fill in some bubbles with the different solutions each of you come up with.

- Use your imagination as you brainstorm new ideas.

- Together, decide which solution will make the biggest difference. Write your group's idea in the solution box. Be sure to use the habit of synergy.

Write Your Idea Here.

The following activities will help you dive into Habit 6. Choose two of them to complete and share your results with someone.

- ⊙ Find a safe international pen-pal club on the Internet and submit your name. This will allow you to get to know people from different cultural backgrounds.

- ⊙ Invite someone from a different cultural background to lunch. Ask about his or her country and unique customs.

- ⊙ Before you turn in your next class writing assignment or project, ask a friend to review it and make suggestions. Be prepared to make changes based on the new insights you receive.

- ⊙ Record any of the above experiences using the Notes feature or this workbook. This will help you keep track of what you learned about synergy.

- ⊙ Review the Baby Steps on p. 202.

Refer to p. 195.

PART 4
Renewal

"TO KEEP A LAMP BURNING, WE HAVE TO KEEP PUTTING OIL IN IT."

—MOTHER TERESA

Habit 7:
Sharpen the Saw

It's about renewing yourself and balancing the key areas of your life: physical, mental, social/ emotional, and spiritual.

Set a timer or alarm for three minutes. Then, in the boxes below, list all of the things you want to do to sharpen your saw in each of the four categories.

BODY (physical)	HEART (relationship)

SOUL (spiritual)	BRAIN (mental)

Refer to p. 208.

ME TIME

Answer each of the questions listed below, then your plan will be set and waiting for you to take action.

What physical activities do you like to do? Are there any activities you haven't tried, but would like to? Make a list.

> Like to do

> Want to try

Choose a few items on your list and write them in the spaces under "Activity" on the chart below.

Decide when, where, and how you will do these activities. Also, write how long you'll spend doing each activity. Involve people who can participate and encourage you to sharpen your saw physically.

ACTIVITY	WHEN, WHERE, HOW	LENGTH OF TIME
Running	Monday and Wednesday in the park with Nina	25 minutes

Print a copy of this chart, save it onto your smart phone or craft your own chart. Just make sure that you keep a copy of it somewhere where you will see it daily.

Refer to p. 208.

Keeping Track

THE BODY

Sharpening the saw physically is not limited just to physical exercise. Think about the food you eat. Answer the following questions, then your plan will be set and waiting for you to take action.

1

What foods did you eat last weekend that were not healthy for your body?

2

How can you change your eating habits?

Use the Notes feature or next page of this workbook to create a plan that will help you focus on good nutritional habits.

Refer to p. 209.

Nutritional Plan

Write Your Nutritional Plan Here.

THE MIND

To care for your brain is to sharpen the saw mentally. Make a list of skills or talents you enjoy or might like to learn.

1

2

3

4

5

Here is another activity to keep your brain sharp:

Interview someone you admire and would like to know more about. Ask about his or her life, challenges, successes, history, and interests. Make your own list of questions below.

Here is an example to get you started:

⊙ What made you decide to become a...?

What did you learn from this interview?

Refer to p. 218.

THE HEART

Caring for your heart is how you sharpen the saw socially and emotionally. Look at it as a Relationship Bank Account. Care for your heart by making deposits. Again, use the Notes feature or this workbook to jot down all the questions.

Add your own ideas of deposits to the list below. BE SPECIFIC.

1. Write a Thank You note to:

Refer to p. 233.

- Which of your relationships are the most important?

- Are you making deposits into these relationships? What are you doing?

- How can you improve your most important relationships?

To boost emotional well-being, why not start your own humor corner today? Write your favorite joke below, then share it with someone.

Write Your Joke Here.

Refer to p. 233.

THE SOUL

Caring for your soul is how you sharpen the saw spiritually. The following activities will help you do this.

> ⊙ Meditate
> ⊙ Volunteer to read to a child for an hour
> ⊙ Listen to inspiring music

What other activities do you enjoy that will help awaken your soul? List them.

ACTIVITY	WHEN, WHERE, HOW	LENGTH OF TIME
Read to a child	Thursday after school, at the hospital	1 hour

Refer to pp. 234-235.

Recap

"IF YOU DO NOT HOPE, YOU WILL NOT FIND WHAT IS BEYOND YOUR HOPES."

– St. Clement of Alexandria

Here is the last page of this Workbook. Now, return to the very beginning and review the personal expectations you wrote down.

Did you meet your expectations? If you feel you didn't, what do you need to do now?

What valuable things did you learn that you didn't expect to learn?

How will you apply the 7 Habits in the next week? Month? Year?

Did you share what you learned? How did it make a difference?

How will you continue to share what you've learned from the 7 Habits?

Record your answers to the above questions using the Notes feature or this workbook.

Write Your Notes Here.

Write Your Notes Here.

Write Your Notes Here.

Write Your Notes Here.

ALSO AVAILIABLE FROM FRANKLINCOVEY

The 6 Most Important Decisions
You'll Ever Make

The 6 Most Important Decisions
You'll Ever Make Workbook

The 7 Habits of Highly Effective Teens

The 7 Habits of Highly Effective Teens
Personal Workbook

The 7 Habits of Highly Effective People

The 7 Habits of Highly Effective Families

The 7 Habits of Happy Kids

The Leader in Me 2nd Edition

The 7 Habits of Highly Effective Teens
Guided Journal

The 7 Habits of Highly Effective Teens:
Habit Tracker

The 7 Habits of Highly Effective Teens on
the Go

For more information on how to bring
The 7 Habits to your school,
visit www.leaderinme.com

www.franklincovey.com
or call 1-800-272-6839

Printed in the USA
CPSIA information can be obtained
at www.ICGtesting.com
JSHW010843300524
64052JS00004B/9

9 781684 816231